Cool Customs

by Janine Scott

Content and Reading Adviser: Mary Beth Fletcher, Ed.D.
Educational Consultant/Reading Specialist
The Carroll School, Lincoln, Massachusetts

Spyglass BOOKS

COMPASS POINT BOOKS

Minneapolis, Minnesota

Compass Point Books
3722 West 50th Street, #115
Minneapolis, MN 55410

Visit Compass Point Books on the Internet at *www.compasspointbooks.com*
or e-mail your request to *custserv@compasspointbooks.com*

Photographs ©: Lindsay Hebberd/Corbis, cover; PhotoSpin, 4; TRIP/B. Seed, 5; TRIP, 6, 7, 15, 19; TRIP/M. Feeney, 8; TRIP/J. Greenberg, 9; TRIP/H. Rogers, 10, 13, 16; Corel, 11, 12, 14; TRIP/M. Barlow, 17, 20; TRIP/M. Jenkin, 18; Brian A. Vikander/Corbis, 21.

Project Manager: Rebecca Weber McEwen
Editor: Heidi Schoof
Photo Researcher: Image Select International Limited
Photo Selectors: Rebecca Weber McEwen and Heidi Schoof
Designers: Les Tranby and Jaime Martens

Library of Congress Cataloging-in-Publication Data

Scott, Janine.
  Cool customs / by Janine Scott ;
      p. cm. — (Spyglass books)
Summary: Provides a brief introduction to customs and traditions
around the world.
Includes bibliographical references and index.
  ISBN 0-7565-0364-7 (hardcover)
  1. Manners and customs—Juvenile literature. [1. Manners and
customs.] I. Title. II. Series.
  GT85 .S26 2002
  390—dc21
                          2002002559

Contents

Spice of Life

Customs are everywhere.
They are in stories, music, arts, and crafts.

They are part of people's food, clothes, and even celebrations.

Did You Know?
A tea ceremony in Japan is quiet. The guests stay silent during part of it.

People in different countries eat different kinds of food.

Meet and Greet

People have different customs in how they greet each other. They may use a hug, kiss, bow, wave, or handshake.

Did You Know?
In New Zealand, a traditional *Maori* greeting is to press noses together.

Festival Fun

Some places have the custom of a festival. Festivals can be in the summer or winter. They can last a day or more than a week.

Did You Know?
In *Bangkok's* Wish Festival, your wish comes true if your candle stays lit as it floats away.

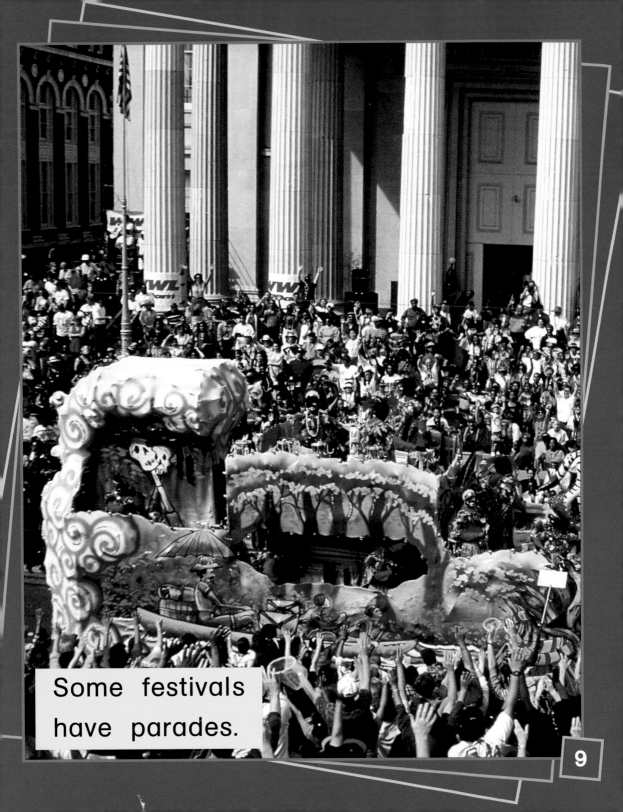

Some festivals have parades.

Music

People everywhere have their own musical customs. Some places have special instruments. Some have special ways of singing.

Did You Know? Steel drums were originally made out of oil barrels.

These Spanish dancers are using *castanets*.

Let's Dance

There are many kinds of dances around the world. They can be slow or fast. Some dancers wear costumes.

Did You Know?

In *Kenya,* men do a dance with long, sharp knives.

These girls are dancing around a May Pole.

Looks Great!

In some places, people decorate their bodies with paint. Some wear fancy jewelry. This can show how powerful or rich they are.

Did You Know?

If someone wears red, it might be to show bravery.

Arts and Crafts

Some people use special patterns and colors on their arts and crafts. Some people are famous for weaving, others for making pots.

Did You Know?
In Japan, cranes and turtles are lucky symbols in art and clothing.

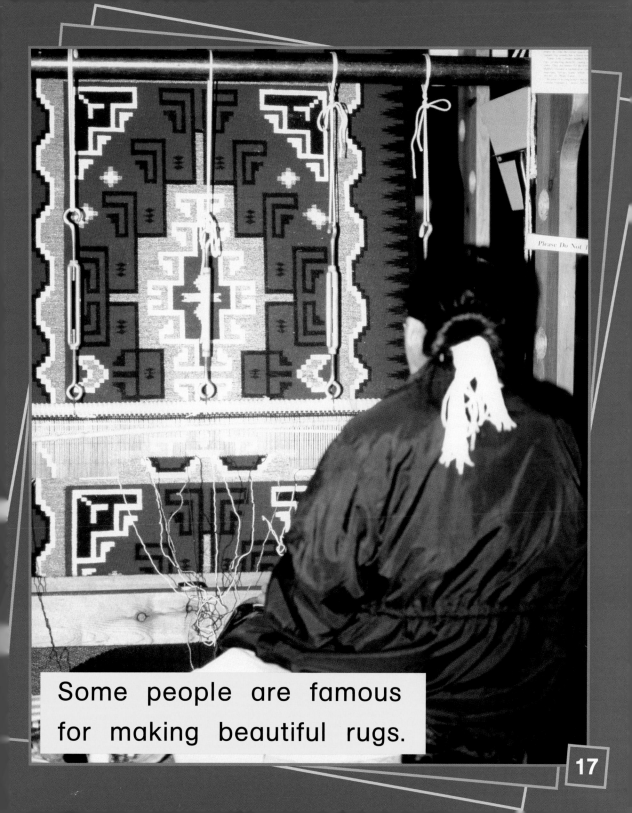

Some people are famous
for making beautiful rugs.

That's the Story

Some people teach their customs by telling stories. These stories can be about animals, brave people, or how Earth was made.

Did You Know?
Sometimes, things tell stories. Totem poles were made to tell family histories.

Built to Last

There are many kinds of homes around the world. Most people build houses that fit the weather where they live. Some people have big families and need big houses.

Did You Know?

In hot, sunny places, houses have thick walls and small windows to keep out the heat.

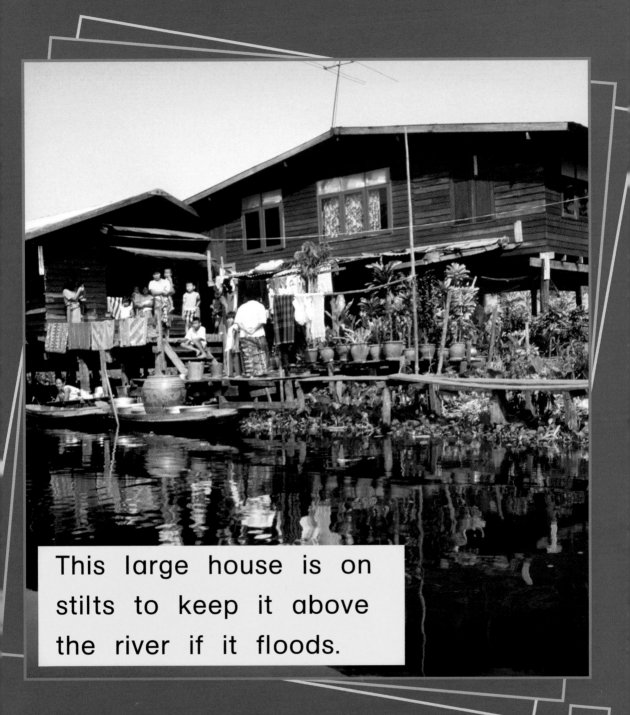

This large house is on stilts to keep it above the river if it floods.

Glossary

Bangkok–a big city in the country called Thailand, which is in Asia

castanets–small hand-held instruments that make a clacking sound

custom–something that people who live in a certain place have been doing for a long time

Kenya–a country on the continent called Africa

Maori–someone or something from the first group of people to live in the country called New Zealand

Learn More

Books

Barmeier, Jim. *Manners and Customs.* New York: Chelsea House Publishers, 1997.

Jeunesse, Gallimard, and Claude Delafosse. *Atlas of People.* New York: Scholastic, 1994.

Luenn, Nancy. *Celebrations of Lights.* Ill. by Mark Bender. New York: Atheneum Books for Young Readers, 1998.

Web Sites

www.nationalgeographic.com/kids/

www.planetpals.com/IKC/Ilearn.html

Index

GR: G
Word Count: 198

From Janine Scott

I live in New Zealand, and have two daughters. They love to read books that are full of fun facts and features. I hope you do, too!